The Animal Within

K͏ATHRINE Y͏ETS

The Animal Within
Copyright © 2021 Kathrine Yets
All Rights Reserved
Published by Unsolicited Press
Printed in the United States of America.
First Edition 2021.

No part of this book may be used or reproduced in any manner whatsoever without written permission except in the case of brief quotations embodied in critical articles or reviews.

A few poems were previously published:
"Kapo-keho-lele" *Fickle Muses*
"Plath's Birthday" Wisconsin Writers Association Jade Ring Award 2018
"Return to Revelations" *Urights*
"Skinny Dipping in Ottowa" *Straylight, Universal Oneness: Magnum Opus Anthology*
"Small Prayer" *Blue Heron Review*
"The river" *Antinarrative* (different form)

Attention schools and businesses: for discounted copies on large orders, please contact the publisher directly. Books are brought to the trade by Ingram.

For information contact:
Unsolicited Press
Portland, Oregon
www.unsolicitedpress.com
orders@unsolicitedpress.com
619-354-8005

Cover Designer: Kathryn Gerhardt
Cover Art: Sarah Richter
Editor: Kristen Marckmann

ISBN: 978-1-950730-98-8

I would like to give thanks to the artists and muses who inspired my ekphrastic works, spiritual search, and found love.

Contents

Bless You	1
Small Prayer	2
King of the Zoo	3
Caught a Crayfish	4
I'm Outta Here	6
Wolf	7
Purple Finch	8
After My Mother's Diagnosis	9
Return to Revelations	10
A Day Depressed at the Zoo	12
Feeling Good	14
Plath's Birthday	16
Kapo-keho-lele	18
The Mermaid	20
Skinny Dipping in Ottawa	23
The river	24
Fall Stream	25
Take me back to six in the morning,	26
Always Only	27
The Animal Within	28

Bless You

Suddenly I realize / That if I stepped out of my body I would break / Into blossom.
—James Wright

Fenced off from the highway,
I gallop in the gleam of the moon.
And the eyes of my two guests
Burst blue at the sight of me.
Their steps plash dew drops
As they breathlessly walk towards me.
My nerves ripple with excitement
As they run their hands through my mane,
Detangle the wind braids of the day.
They lift their heads boldly as sunflowers.
There is no bliss like theirs.
I nudge one's hand with my muzzle,
To welcome him into my home, my pasture,
Invite him to graze with me under sable skies.
His fingertips kiss my ear,
As soft as a tired saddle.
Suddenly, he freezes in time.
His face opens like a lysianthus.

Small Prayer

And then there was a hummingbird,
aqua breasts and grey wings,
without a sky to fly in.

But there was a rose tightly closed,
which teased its tongue; its beak,
creased from years of use,
unable to bend just right.

And I prayed for this bird.
Prayed the rose would open
just a few days sooner,
expose its nectar
like a woman
separating her lips just right—
one could only wish to kiss them
even before she speaks.

King of the Zoo

Inspired in part by William Blake's "Tyger"

Lyon! Lyon! lying down,
Yawning at the crowd around
What living thing captured through lens
Could look more caged than you?

Which exhibit or which zoo
Stole the wild from your eyes?
Tamed your mane without a comb?
Stopped the roar within your throat?

Were you born in captivity?
Taught to deny proclivity?
What put your jaw in such a drowse?
Your claw into such a daze?

Who dared to numb your instinct?
Who filed down your thirty teeth?
Turned your snarl into a snivel?
Who broke you?

Lyon! Lyon! lying down,
Yawning at the crowd around,
What living thing captured through lens
Could look more caged than you?

Caught a Crayfish

Age six and unafraid
of whatever squirms in pond scum.
But crawdaddies' claws get to me.
It scares me when they creak open,
click together like barber blades.

I hold its slick body
tight between my fingers.
Its feather gills flare out—
I freak out, throw it
down into the grass.

Polished black pebbles
look up at me.
Its claws go up and down,
like it's about to conduct an orchestra.
A melody comes to my head,
I begin to hum "Under the Sea."
Mosquitoes buzz in harmony,
bullfrogs croak the beat.

Sebastian,
I call it.

Its claws reach up towards me,
Pick me up, I hear it say.
My hand fans open to grab.

I hear the creak, then a click-
snip right into my pinky.
Blood gushes through my fantasy.

I'm Outta Here

One hand on the rein braid,
        callous in my palm—
ground flesh from flesh.
        My free hand waves willy-nilly
to the screaming crowd.

Gelding's been straight line buckin'—
        Time to switch it up,
escapes through my gritted teeth.

        I press hard on the stirrups.
8 seconds, no less—
        each as long as a timber rattler.
He veers a furious left,
        bows,
then bucks up his back legs.

Wolf

Ahhwoooo at the full
strawberry harvest moon in June
and breath in the sweet smells of midnight's squalor,
where the fields are bare of bristling beasts
besides the one lone *ahhwwooo* on the wind
that wisps through blades of grass, across woods, above ponds,
but is heard by no one at all.

Purple Finch

Patriarch's red throat
gushes—bleeds above
heads of broods.

Their palates exposed,
ready to consume,
receive communion he allows.

Purge desire down their throat,
teach them what to have an appetite for
in their white bellies.

He warbles near their nest
a lullaby of restrictions.

After My Mother's Diagnosis

Cat, my mother says, then I arch my back on all fours.
Cow, she says next, so I slope my spine.
She teaches me words like when I was five.
Become parallel with the floor, she corrects,
then praises, *perfect Plow!*
I go into Warrior without direction,
bend down to Dancing, look up at her smile
through my splayed fingers.
 Then she covers her eyes and sighs.
Guide yourself in meditation.

Without her, I go into my heart
and find emerald green fading to pear.
A single chime mimes the dissipate
of my mother walking away.

Return to Revelations

*If you eat a flower
you will return to that place someday,*
my mother told me, age five.
Her pink hibiscus took her back to Hawaii.
My wild violets always took me
back to my grandparents' home.

They're good for your heart, Grandpa said months after
returning from the hospital,
his heart still weak.
I picked unblemished bunches from the side of his garage
to share with him, to strengthen us both.
Purple crunched between our teeth
with a subtle sweetness.

Over a decade later, we share asparagus—
steamed, soft, green.
It can cure cancer,
he told me— proved with an article.
Unnecessary, I believe.
He buys me bunches from Pick 'n Save.
3 tbsp a day, at least.

While eating, he speaks of Revelations,
Redemption is in your lifetime.
Christ will come to your generation, Katie.
I cling to his every word,
but do not hold it as my own.

In the following hour I learn
there is no hell, no heaven either.
There is only sleep.
We wait.
Just look in the Bible, it's all there.
We will all return . . . heaven's on earth.

He hands me Tupperware as I leave.
I deny it; try to make him keep his green cure.
Try to make him save himself.
Just take it.
I do. My hands suddenly smaller
and filled with wild violets.

A Day Depressed at the Zoo

How many people cry at the zoo per day?
I feel like a mason jar,
fragile and useless,
as I pass through the crowd.
A true novelty just like the rest of them.

I realize how spoiled I am—
I can have water when I want it.
A woman in her hijab cries by the bubbler
to her mother, who knows why,
but I guess. Kids crawling all around her.
A whole different animal I can't even handle.

The world is talking to me in Morse code,
but I can't understand it.
The peacock cries out, screaming like my mother.
And I'm listening to my sister
complain about her wedding,
which will be held in the monkey exhibit next spring.

The world speaks, but I don't understand.
The hippo wiggles its ears, and the albino giraffe
makes a noise I can't even describe.
Here I am in the middle like a prairie dog

without a hole, scorched by August's sun,
hungover without water, wondering
how to make sense of my surroundings.

I run through the zoo to meet my mother
to go to therapy and get more drugs.
$500 for 30 pills, yes, the price of happiness
is high these days, and I wonder why
I can't be that girl with the purple hair
I just passed, who smiles and laughs
like a lion while I'm running
through the middle of a crowd
tears blurring my eyes without reason.
I wonder how many people cry at the zoo per day.

Feeling Good

"It is always the result of mental "static"—distortions. Your blue mood can be compared to the scratchy music coming from a radio. The problem is not that the tubes or transistors are blown out or defective, or that the signal from the radio station is distorted as a result of bad weather. You just simply have to adjust the dials. When you learn to bring about this mental tuning, the music will come through clearly again and your depression will lift."

—David Burns

As natural to you as the way you hold your fork,
you tell yourself over and over
that you deserve to die.
And while your perfectionist ass keeps
picking your scabs,
the rest of the world stops bleeding.

Wake up.
There is no dichotomy within the dust on the floor,
and today's failure will be next week's broken plate
but only if you let it.
Stop holding your hair dryer over the tub.
Quit contemplating swallowing your jasper stone.
Tomorrow will come with its dishes
and boxes of clothes from the move
you refuse to put away.

Tomorrow will come with its garden full of weeds
and sun burning your face to cancer.

Stop.
Breathe.
You are glorious in your ways
when you walk across the stone path
to your car each morning—
your hips swaying as the bone curves.
There is hydrangea just outside your window, as blue as the sky
you fail to see each day.
Look up. Look down. Look somewhere besides within yourself.

The lion of emotions lies in the pit of your stomach,
(which roars because your appetite is obsolete).
Ignore it.
Let it go.
Let your mind see the Pacific Ocean at midnight
as you wade in wearing your little black dress.
Think of swing sets on an overcast day.
What is happiness? you keep asking.
It's not within your heart anymore, so look around.
There are fireflies waiting for you.
Listen for their wings' flap.

Plath's Birthday

"Nobody in the lane, / And nothing, nothing but blackberries."
—Sylvia Plath

Nothing but pumpkins left to right
With ivy swirls, curls around my boots, and a cornfield
Somewhere at the end of it, mazing. Pumpkins
Big as my head, fat
With star glisten seeds and guts.
I had not asked for such orange,
Burnt as the ember of my cigarette. They love me;
They wait for picking like girls at a bar or dance.

Overhead, the crows caw—
Theirs is the voice of Autumn,
Of pumpkin ale and cranberry moonshine—
Bits of last night's ashes in the sky.
I come to one patch of pumpkins, so bright it hurts my eyes,
Slumping their amber bellies and their knotted stems in a
haystack.
I believe in a kind of heaven with one look—
Hooked into this moment in October.

The only thing to come now is the cornfield
Between two hills. The wind blows and a stalk
Slaps me like a playful lover.
These hills, these fields once too green and sweet
To know the bitter pumpkin seed.
I follow a scarecrow's path to the hill's southern face,
And the face is gold,
That looks out on nothing, nothing but wheat and grass
And the occasional stray cow, lowing.

Kapo-keho-lele

I drift across the ocean
above a lava coral reef
this blue skied noon.
I hear a cry echo from the shore.

My sister needs me. Pele.
I feel hands around her throat.
Her ti leaf dress being torn.
Her hair ripped from the root.

I fly fast to where she lies
and find her beneath Kamapua'a,
the pig himself—half hog, half man, all lust.
My sister cries, he grunts.

I address the beast,
I am the sacred night, streaked with dark,
darker than the deepest depths of the Pacific.
Red-spotted magic of your nightmares.

Ravisher, beware. I am the red eel woman.
Sorcerous demon of desire.
You defile my sister, defile the goddess of fire.
And so you will be damned.

Words do not stir the beast,
so I wield my keo-lele
and cast my sweet scent past his nose.
Hook, line, sucker.

He chases and chases
my flying yoni past Hanauma Bay,
round Koʻolau Volcano,
and crashes so hard he creates a crater.

Pleased with my yoni,
I place it back under my hibiscus skirt
and dance Laka's sacred hula
with my sister; the sun drying her tears.

The Mermaid

I
I see her near the water; her chest
covered by jingle shells,
shimmering light pink in the moonlight.
She sings a hushed lullaby that travels on the wind
like an orca's echo in the ocean.
And my heart pours from my throat for her—
a lonesome duet
floods the beach until the horizon turns roseate.

II
Her eyes are gold medallions in the sun.
The tail flames fuchsia
with each scale speckled by sand-diamonds.
In awe, I step closer.
The dawn exposes me as a stranger,
feet instead of fins.
The gold glint of her eyes turns copper
before she flips into the tide.
I cannot follow.

III
I paddle a rowboat out at midnight in a mist,
spotlighting the waters by lantern.
If only I could remember our melody,
then she would surface.
I hear a plash past starboard,

so I peer into the gray—nothing.
Certain I see a glimpse of fanned fuchsia.
Perhaps a mirage in peripherals.

IV
Three days I sought her without luck.
Now I sit, legs dangling off the dock,
singing Haul Away Joe in monotone.
A hum follows the salt breeze, a faint purl in the water.
Morgan, I murmur, as sailors would call her.
Again, *Morgan,* seeps from my lips,
and there she is—
her dark auburn hair glassed
and tousled by waves.
I dive in.

V
My sundress blooms up like a mushroom
around me,
and I writhe, swimming toward
where I last saw her.
Feel a tickle on my ankle,
then a tug, then suddenly, I am submerged.
My vision blurs, all I see is auburn
and fuchsia swirls, gleaming past me.
I close my eyes, let the water take me,
and feel a ripple tingle my lips.

VI
Her scales smooth against my thighs,
I wrap around her, pull her deeper

into our kiss; her lips soft as cyclamen.
She breathes into me and gives new life:
eyes of silver, fins of turquoise and cerulean.
She cups my breasts with calico scallops
then traces her fingers down my navel
to my tail, which swishes at her touch.

Skinny Dipping in Ottawa

It was dark.
Every longing star in the sky
reflected on the placid water,
begging to be touched.
I stepped into this galaxy—
as quiet as you would expect it to be—
sending a ripple through the moon.

Water trickled off my skin.
Liquid wind chimes,
each drop had its own note to play.

I moved among the stars till I was submerged;
a part of this sky but distinct from it.
I let the water take me,
hold me up between two worlds,
float between two skies.

The river

The sky is tufts of cobalt and grey.
The reeds sway and I'm reminded of 5 years ago,
sitting on the park bench writing about love.
I now know love is not
a silver Audi or a lavender carnation.
It's inside me.
It's the sway of my hips and the hue of my lips.
It's outside of me.
The murky Fox River and the bench
covered with moss.
Love whispers like a prayer in church on a Tuesday
afternoon and smells like vodka when it's between two.
There isn't enough love within this poem for more than just the
        river.

Fall Stream

flows without sound.
Red oak leaves give a speech
about where these branches have been.
They have touched summer's
pure apricot hair with their tips.

But the stream has no reply,
no incite.
Maneuvers around rocks aimless
because there is nowhere to go,
but there is someone to see.

Green—there is still green
with roots that reach through mud
to drink in the silence.
The stream has no objection.

What can be said without sound?
No shape to gesture?
The stream can only mimic in reflections,
give what is already there.

Take me back to six in the morning,

fishing for patience.
Forget 9 to 5.
Give me a sky I can taste,
cup in my hands, splash on my face—
wake up
and don't go to work.
Go to a lake. Arrive a half hour later
than planned. Walk to the dock.
Cast.
Sit back and don't wonder
about the paperwork on your desk,
about the emails,
about the hospital bills . . .
Stop. A boat rumbles a ways from shore
and makes my lure jump in the tide.
Rest in this world.

Always Only

Always only your flesh
under my nails. The hope rising
inside my chest. Always
only yours, the waves
we make between thighs
high as clouds, loud
as wolves' howls. I
viciously in vain try
to consume you
become one and whole
but we are two beings,
my love—Always only.

The Animal Within

There is a roar caught in your throat
each morning before the coffee
and scrambled eggs with pepper.
There are stretch marks down your spine—
tiger stripes.
There is a lion in his snores
that keep you awake
until I am.
There is a snarl between his teeth
as you kiss his bottom lip.
There are scratch marks down his back,
across his chest from when you
both let out the animal within.

About the Author

Kathrine Yets lives in St. Francis, WI and teaches secondary English. She recently won the Jade Ring Award from the Wisconsin Writers' Association for her poem "Plath's Birthday." Her work can be found in *River&South Review, FishFood Magazine, Fickle Muses,* and elsewhere. When she is not writing or teaching, she can be found in the park reading or napping.

About the Press

Unsolicited Press was established in 2012 and is based in Portland, Oregon. The team produces poetry, fiction, and nonfiction by award-winning and emerging writers.

Learn more at www.unsolicitedpress.com.

www.ingramcontent.com/pod-product-compliance
Lightning Source LLC
Chambersburg PA
CBHW030142100526
44592CB00011B/1008